D0358974

The life cycle of a
Bean

Ruth Thomson

WAYLAND

First published in 2007 by Wayland
an imprint of Hachette Children's Books

Copyright © Wayland 2007

British Library Cataloguing in Publication Data
Thomson, Ruth
  The life cycle of a bean. - (Learning About Life Cycles)
  I. Beans - Life cycles - Juvenile literature
I Title
571.8'2374

ISBN-13: 9780750248624
ISBN-10: 0750248629

Editor: Victoria Brooker
Designer: Simon Morse
Senior Design Manager: Rosamund Saunders

Printed and bound in China

Hachette Children's Books
A division of Hodder Headline Limited
338 Euston Road, London NW1 3BH

Photographs: All cover images and 1, 4-5,
8, 9, 10, 11, 12, 13, 14, 16, 17, 20, 21, 23
Adam White/naturepl.com; 6 Geoff Dann/
DK Images; 7 Roger Phillips/DK Images;
13 Oxford Scientific Films; 15 Premaphoto/
naturepl.com; 18 John B. Free/naturepl.com;
19Meul/ARCO/naturepl.com;
22 wikipedia/nl:Gebruiker:Rasbak

Contents

Beans grow here

Broad beans are good to eat. People grow them in their gardens or **allotments**. Farmers grow thousands of broad bean plants in enormous fields.

What is a broad bean?

A broad bean is a **seed**. Several grow
together inside a pod. The tough, thick
skin of the pod protects
the beans. The beans
we eat are soft
and green.

pod

bean

This is what a bean looks like inside.

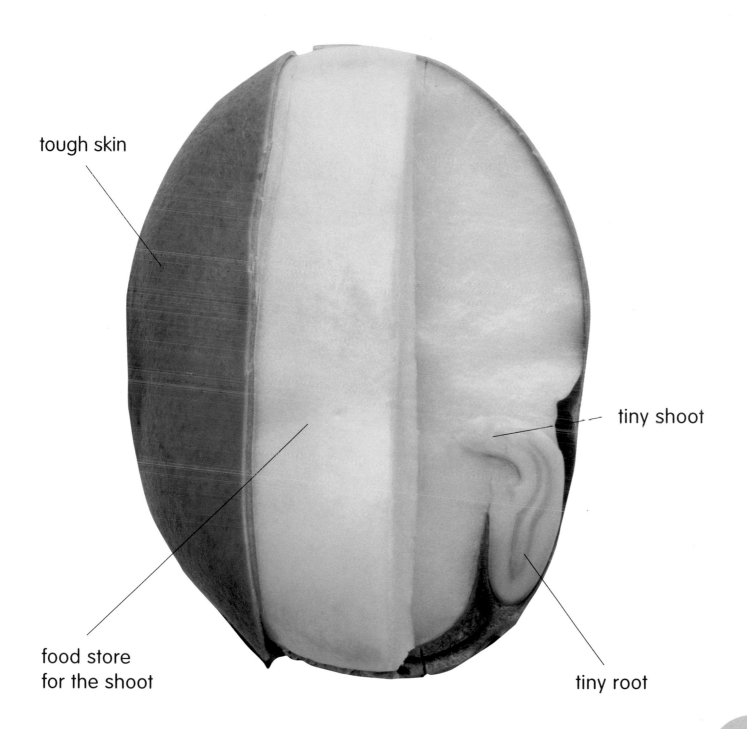

tough skin

tiny shoot

food store
for the shoot

tiny root

Planting

People save a store of beans as seeds for planting. They leave the beans to dry. The beans turn hard and brown.

In springtime,
the beans are
planted in warm, damp soil.
Water makes the beans swell.

Roots

The hard skin of the bean splits.

A tiny **root** pokes out.

It starts to grow

down into

the soil.

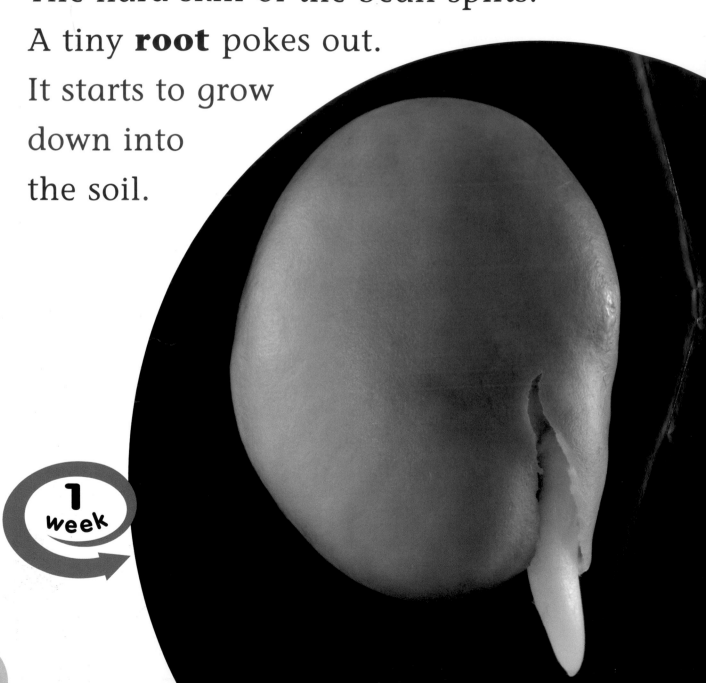

1 week

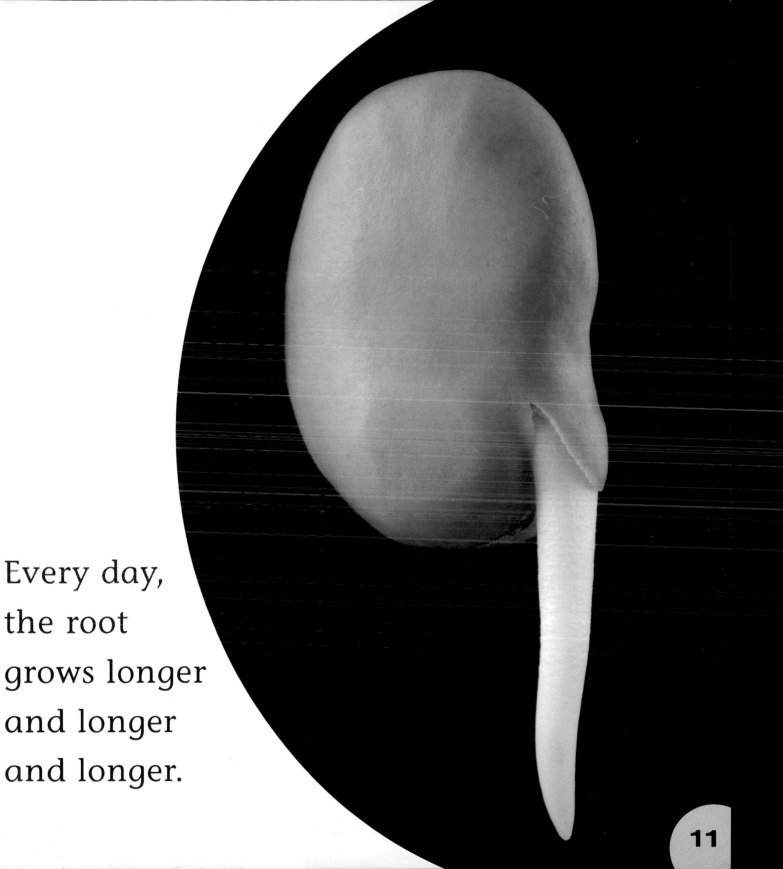

Every day,
the root
grows longer
and longer
and longer.

11

Shoot

A **shoot** starts to grow upwards. On its tip are tiny **leaves**. These bend downwards, so they do not break as the shoot pushes through the soil.

2 weeks

The shoot pops out of the soil. The leaves uncurl and turn darker. Side **roots** grow from the main root. Tiny hairs on them take up water from the soil.

3 weeks

6 weeks

Leaves

Now the plant has used up the bean's food store. The **leaves** spread out to catch sunlight. Leaves use water from the soil, sunlight and air to make food.

Blackfly lay their eggs on the leaves. When the young **hatch,** they eat the leaves. Ladybirds gobble up blackfly, so the leaves do not become too damaged.

10
weeks

Flowers

Every week the plant grows taller and the **leaves** grow bigger. Flower **buds** begin to form.

The buds open out into white flowers.
In the centre of each flower
are tiny grains of yellow **pollen** and
a sweet liquid called **nectar**.

12
weeks

Pollination

Bees crawl inside the flowers to sip the **nectar** and collect the **pollen**. The black lines on the petals point the way to the nectar.

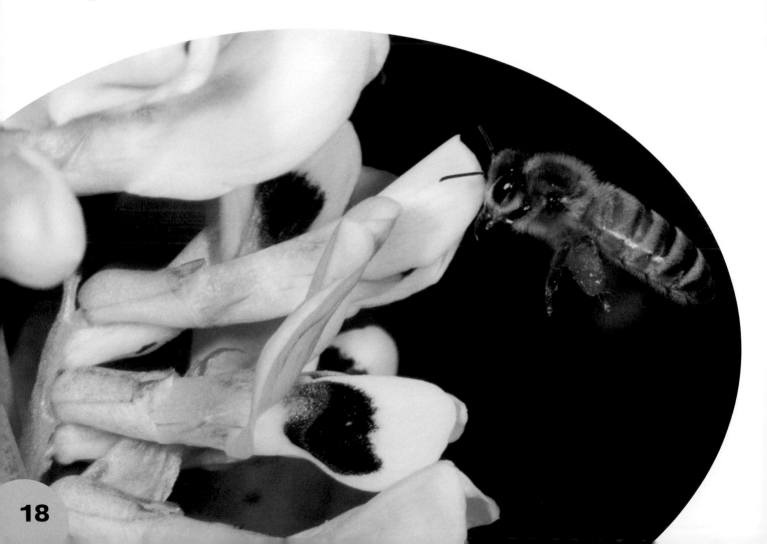

As a bee flies from
one flower to another, pollen sticks
onto its hairy legs. Pollen from one
flower rubs off onto the next one.
This pollen helps to make new beans.

Beans

Now the flower is no longer needed.
Its petals **wither** and fall off,
leaving a pod with tiny beans inside.

14 weeks

The beans swell and grow. The pods become long and heavy. People pick the pods before the beans are fully grown, when they are tastiest.

18-20 weeks

24 weeks

New seeds

In the autumn, the bean plant shrivels and dies. Unpicked pods turn brown and fall to the ground. Some beans are collected for planting next spring.

Bean life cycle

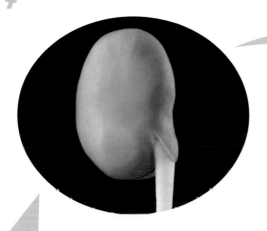

Bean
The bean is planted. After 1 week a **root** grows.

Leaves
A **shoot** grows up out of the soil. The **leaves** uncurl.

Bean pods
After 18 weeks, the beans are ready to be picked.

Flowers
The plant grows taller and after 12 weeks flowers appear.

Glossary

allotment a small piece of land that people rent for growing plants

bud a swelling on a stem that will grow into a flower or leaves

leaves the part of a plant that makes food

nectar the sweet juice inside a flower

pollen the grains of powder in the centre of a flower

root the underground part of a plant which takes in water from the soil

seed the part of a plant that grows into a new plant

shoot the first leaves of a new plant

wither shrink and dry up

Index